MY TOURETTE

Written by Tristan D. Reese
Illustrated by Yelka Y. Reese

DEDICATION

I dedicate this book first to God for giving me the strength to face each day. Secondly, to my brother Hayden who is my biggest fan and my parents. Especially my mom who spent countless hours helping me put my book together. Thank you for loving me, encouraging me and just letting me be myself.

I also dedicate this book to every kid who gets the chance to read it.

Hello, my name is Tristan. I am 10 years old and I am a kid just like you. Except, I have something called Tourette Syndrome.

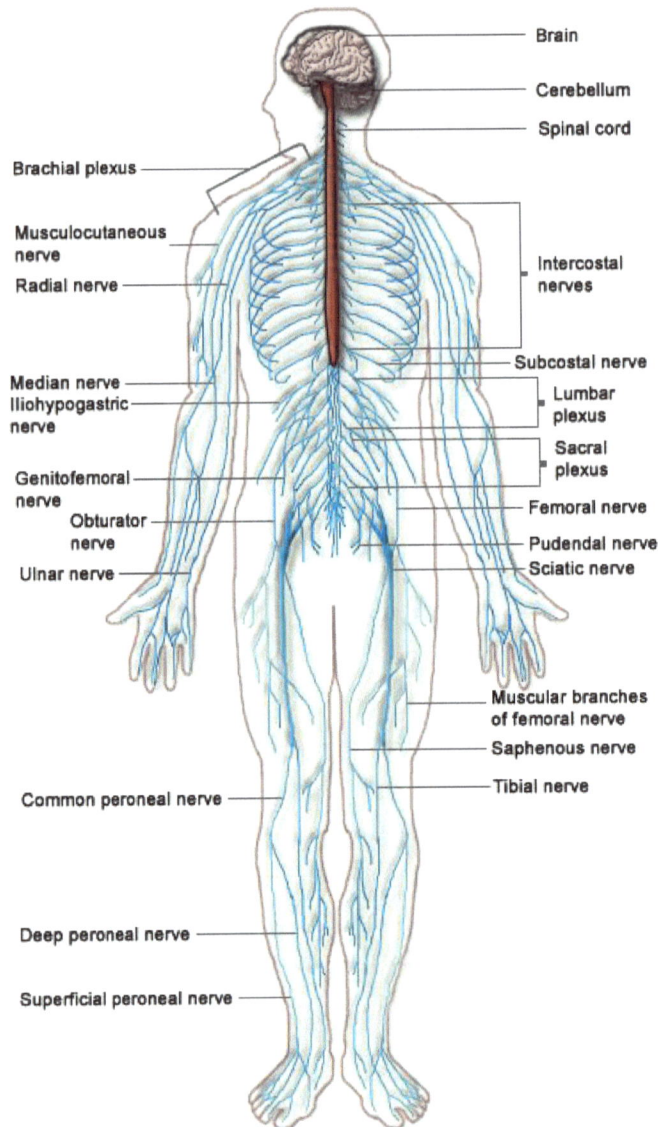

Brain

Cerebellum

Spinal cord

Brachial plexus

Musculocutaneous nerve

Radial nerve

Intercostal nerves

Subcostal nerve

Median nerve

Iliohypogastric nerve

Lumbar plexus

Sacral plexus

Genitofemoral nerve

Obturator nerve

Femoral nerve

Pudendal nerve

Sciatic nerve

Ulnar nerve

Muscular branches of femoral nerve

Saphenous nerve

Tibial nerve

Common peroneal nerve

Deep peroneal nerve

Superficial peroneal nerve

Tourette Syndrome is a medical condition that affects the nervous system. Children and adults with Tourette Syndrome have tics. Tics are sudden movements or sounds that a person with Tourette Syndrome cannot stop from happening. It is something I was born with. It can be very hard to be a kid with Tourette Syndrome. People with Tourette Syndrome do not choose to have it and they did not do anything bad or wrong to cause them to get it. Tourette Syndrome is hereditary, it is passed down in your genes and you have it for your entire life.

About 148,000 kids in the United States have Tourette Syndrome. Most kids with Tourette Syndrome usually don't start showing tics until between the ages of 5 and 8 years old. I started showing my tics at the age of 2.

Kids with Tourette Syndrome are just like all other kids. We love to do all the things other kids do.

I love to go kayaking with my dad and...

spend time with my brother at the petting zoo...

and I especially love the beach.

Living with Tourette Syndrome is very hard. It makes my body do things that I cannot control or stop. It's like a hiccup that never goes away. It is like being tossed on a roller coaster ride that never ends. It is a part of me that I cannot separate from. It is something that makes my body do things that I cannot control. Just like you cannot stop yourself from blinking, I cannot stop my body from making noises or moving. It is something that can be very hard to make other people understand.

Sometimes, when grown ups or kids do not know what I have, they may get upset with me because they think that I may be doing things on purpose. This really makes me feel sad and makes me wish that I could stop my tics. Unfortunately, there is no cure for Tourette Syndrome but there are medications that may help make my tics less frequent.

Sometimes when my tics start happening, I try to hold my body to stop myself from moving.

I have many tics, they include: opening my mouth as wide as I can, blinking, sniffing things, twitching my nose, touching things, shrugging my shoulders, clearing my throat, singing songs or saying words over and over again. Tics make me move my body all the time, especially my hands, legs and feet. They also make me jump, cough, kick, scream, stick my tongue out, bite it, suck my teeth, move my neck back as far as I can, stretch my whole body, shake my head, crack my toes, knuckles and back. I also make very high pitch sounds and very low growl sounds when I am upset, annoyed, frustrated or stressed. Also, my movements and my noises change all the time. However, there are times my movements give me comfort.

There are times when my tics are happening, that people will look at me in a funny way. Which makes me feel really uncomfortable.

The worse part of having Tourette Syndrome is the stress of dealing with it everyday. I don't always know what my body will do and I get a lot of Stress headaches that last for days, sometimes weeks. There are times when all my tics tend to "speed up" because they occur too often and too much. I try to channel my stress and suppress my tics using all my strength but I wind up with a headache. I can only keep them from happening for a little while but within a couple of minutes or a couple of hours, they let loose. I wish I could stop.

When the stress is too much, I calm myself down with sheer will power or music. I listen a lot to Judy Jacobs, who is a gospel singer. I also play the piano and the trumpet. These things make my tics go away for a while. My tics also seem to slow down when I am reading or in deep thought. Doing artistic things also help.

In spite of my Tourette Syndrome, I have accomplished many things. I learned acrobatics and gymnastics. I have taken swimming and martial arts; I play the trumpet and the piano. I won an award for a science project and I have been in a couple of plays in my town. My mom always tells me that Tourette Syndrome cannot stop me from accomplishing what I want to do in life. That if I believe it, I can achieve it. I know this to be true because there are many famous people with Tourette Syndrome. People like; Steve Wallace - NASCAR Driver, Eric Bernotas - US Olympic Bobsledder, Tim Howard - famous Soccer Player, Jim Eisenreich - Major League Baseball Player, Dan Ackroyd and Dash Mihok – both famous Actors and Michael Wolff, a famous Jazz musician, composer and producer.

So, even though I have Tourette Syndrome, I am more than just a 10-year-old kid with Tourette. I go to school, I have friends, I am pretty artistic, neat, smart and strong. I am also very fast and athletic. Best of all, I have a family who loves me just as I am.

Conditions like Tourette Syndrome can be very difficult for anyone to live with. If you want to help kids that have Tourette Syndrome or any type of disability, you can help by trying to learn more about them. By being understanding and patient with anyone who is different and encouraging other kids to do the same. If you see someone being mistreated for any reason, speak up.

AFTERWORD

Living with Tourette Syndrome has been very challenging for me and my family. School can be very difficult at times because of my condition. One of the reasons that I wrote this book was because my tics became more intense and the other kids in my class were having a hard time understanding my situation. My mom suggested that I write down how I felt so that I could share it with the other kids in my class and help them to understand what Tourette Syndrome is and what I have to go through everyday. I turned my writing into this book.

I also wrote this book because I wanted to raise awareness about Tourette Syndrome, wherever and whenever this book is read. After writing my book, I got a chance to read it to the entire fifth grade in my school. I received a lot of great positive responses. A lot of the kids said that they finally understood why I did certain things. They also asked me a lot of questions and I answered them as best as I could. Reading my book to all my classmates was very therapeutic for me. I was finally able to express to everyone what I was going through for so long.

EXTRA

These are some of the questions I answered after I read my book to my classmates:

1. Who helped you understand Tourette Syndrome?
   My mom.

2. Do you know when your tics are about to happen?
   Yes.

3. Do you notice when they are happening?
   Yes.

4. How long do tics usually last?
   Each tic is about a few seconds but they happen continuously so it feels like a long time.

5. What is the longest tic you have had?
   20 minutes.

6. If you break a body part (like an arm or a leg) do tics affect the broken part?
   I am not sure but the broken part is kind of "disconnected" so I don't think it would be affected by the tics.

7. If you get angry, how do tics affect you?
   They get worse. There are more of them and they start happening faster.

8. **When a tic is about to happen, do you ever try to hide it?**
   Yes.

9. **Is there something that helps stop tics?**
   There are different medications that can be used to help people with Tourette. They do help to slow down the tics but they don't take them completely away.

10. **Are there some medicines that works better than other medicines to help stop the tics?**
    Yes. Some TS medicines work better than others but not all TS medicines work the same for everyone who has TS.

11. **Can Tourette Syndrome medicine be used for anything other than Tourette?**
    Yes. Some of the medications used to treat people with Tourette Syndrome are actually used to treat other things as well. I use Clonidine, which is also used to treat high blood pressure, migraine headaches and other conditions.

12. **Does Tourette syndrome affect you while you're sleeping?**
    Yes. I move around a lot when I sleep, which makes me really tired in the morning.

13. **Do you grow out of tics?**

    Tics can slow down as you get older for some people with Tourette but they usually don't go away for good.

14. **How does Tourette affect the things you do everyday, like homework?**

    It can be very hard to do some things at times because my tics make it hard to concentrate.

15. **How does your family help you deal with your Tourette Syndrome?**

    They are very understanding and they let me be myself all over the house. I don't have to try to hold my tics when I am with them. My parents also made a space for me to exercise in the house for when my tics become too much for me.

RESOURCES

For more information about Tourette Syndrome visit the following websites:

www.tsa-usa.org

www.tourettesyndrome.net

www.ninds.nih.gov

kidshealth.org

If your child is being bullied because of a disability or any other reason, please visit these websites for more information on what you can do.

www.stopbullyingnow.hrsa.gov

www.stompoutbullying.org

www.stopbullying.gov/kids

www.stopbullyingnowfoundation.org

No kid is an island and you should not have to go it alone. If you are being bullied or know someone who is, speak up, be a friend and tell an adult who is able to help.

SPECIAL THANKS

I want to give a very special thank you to my teacher, Mrs. Mahoney for allowing me to read my book to the class and for all her help and support during the school year.

www.ingramcontent.com/pod-product-compliance
Lightning Source LLC
Chambersburg PA
CBHW042128040426
42450CB00002B/120